Pink Gems

Dominique D. Glisson

Pink Gems

The Pink Trilogy (Part 3)

By

Dominique D. Glisson

Founder and CEO of AfroSoFly Inc.

Cover Design: "Sacred Queen" by Chris Anderson

COPYRIGHT ©2021 DOMINIQUE D. GLISSON

ALL RIGHTS RESERVED

All rights reserved. No part of this publication may be reproduced, distributed, or transmitted in any form or by any means, including photocopying, recording, or other electronic or mechanical methods, without the prior written permission of the publisher, except in the case of brief quotations embodied in critical reviews and certain other noncommercial uses permitted by copyright law. For permission requests, contact the publisher at the email below.

AFROSOFLY PUBLISHING, LLC

info@afrosofly.com

www.afrosofly.com

ISBN
978-1-7349245-3-4

Ordering Information:

Special discounts are available on quantity purchases by corporations, associations and others. For details, contact the publisher at the email address below.

To book Dominique D. Glisson for an interview, speaking engagement or private event, please email: dominique@kahawia.com.

Dedicated
to
those
who
never
forgot
to
remember
me.

Something Like a Love Letter

Self-love doesn't always come with flowers.
Sometimes it's standing in front of the mirror,
glossy-eyed, with every urge to cry
and still pleading with self to say something nice.
What starts as a cracked whisper
is now a matter of bathroom trial.
Can you convince yourself,
beyond a reasonable doubt,
that the love you feel for self is real?
Self-love isn't always positive affirmations.
Many times it's just breathing.
To stay in bed or to get out of bed?
Better to choose between those two
than to love yourself to death
—today; tonight.
Self-love isn't always difficult.
On a rare occasion, it just flows…

A woman with many names,
I am the reason I strive to be better.
Better than I was 20 years ago
and better than I'm destined to be.
I am the fuel that revs my drive
to reach the ultimate lifestyle that I desire.
Since '89, I've been the truest
version of myself for myself.

Pink Gems   *Creative*

I've held my own hand
through mud, gravel and all the storms.
With my back straight and my head high,
I stand 10 toes down and 12 feet tall.
I tower over small minded folks
that try to run up on me.
Can't count the number of times
I've stood my ground
and repositioned my crown
in the faces of friends and frenemies alike.
I am everything
a mother could want her daughter to be
—even with my flaws.
I am a Goddess;
skin of bronze dipped in mango butter.
My curves are the compass
of my body's roadmap.
Dare to be led
to the depth of my love
as told by my eyes;
or check for my beauty
in the stretch marks on my thighs.
I am a Queen
with one of the most beautiful souls
to ever walk the streets.
So fierce,
I'm sure I make the devil nervous.
I cuss, pray and speak life

Pink Gems   *Sincere*

—all with the same tongue.
The Most High has vested the power in me
to transform the energy
of my inner G
into wisdom for those who need it
and to breathe havoc on those who've earned it.
I wish a muhfucka would give me a reason;
as I am both analytical and creative
plus 3 scoops of provocative.
My ancestors are not
guiding me to play with ya'll.
I am
ButtaFlyy
Kahawia
Domo
Nique Nique
Sticks
Dom
Dominique
Desiree
Glisson
—I love all of me.

Pink Gems *Confident*

You Can't Sit with Me

You can't sit with me.
For the duration of my entire life,
I've been granting people access to me.
I've provided countless opportunities
to folks who've never paid their dues.
Never again.
I'm here to let you know up front—
You can't sit with me.
I am the CEO of my life
and every high-ranking organization has its criteria.
The times for being any old Joe Schmo
with smiles, kind words and empty commitments
wrapped up in glossy paper are over.
In order to consider yourself a member,
you must apply yourself.
Apply yourself to the enhancement
of Dominique Glisson Inc.
Ain't no lingering around to get a seat at my table.
You need to have your own
—table, that is.
You need to be able to provide
the basics for self
or else, you can't sit with me.
You need to have a vision
cuz Sis ain't got time for dreams.
Sis ain't got time

Pink Gems   *Diligent*

for those who don't help themselves.
Sis ain't got time
for folks with no goals;
folks with no clear outline of the pathway ahead;
folks who don't know themselves;
folks who play around with time;
folks who beg for support
but never show and prove;
folks who only show up
when the cameras are rolling;
folks who only talk cuz they got lips;
folks whose contributions to my energy
are forever unmatched.
Sis ain't got time.
It's me.
I'm Sis.
You can't sit with me.

Pink Gems *Generous*

Flower Shower

Roses are for regular folks,
I prefer the lotus.
It blooms pretty like my pussy.
and you should already know this.
Know it like you know my smell.
Know it like you know my name.
Know it like you know
a thunderstorm gets wetter
than regular ass rain.
Lotus petals,
soft like my lips.
Whether face or nether,
they both deserve a kiss.
See, I'm not a regular-degular
shawtii from around the way;
I'm a Queen from Kings County
and I got time today.
Time for you to suck my toes
and make me climb the walls.
Time to introduce your dick to my tonsils
while I lick your balls.
Time for you to make the nape of my neck
connect with the back of my knees.
Time for you to stick the tip in and pull it out
—make me beg for it, please!

Pink Gems *Passionate*

Twisted Promise

You've promised me many things
when all I ever asked
is for you to be yourself.
Your true self.
Not the made up version
of the man you created in your head.
I told you from day 1
that I don't believe in promises.
Promises are merely jokes
without the laughter attached.
Except, that last laugh
is always lingering somewhere.
All I asked was that you reveal
your true intentions.
Hell, I shared mine with you.
I told you on day 2
that I was only interested
in having a mutual affair.
A sexual agreement in which I would
only call on you to satisfy my needs.
On day 3, I asked
if you knew how to tie a knot?
It was then you promised me
that I wouldn't be able to escape it.
Yet, here I am
spread eagle across the dinner table.

Pink Gems   *Beautiful*

My wrists aren't correctly tied to my ankles
—even with the duct tape
doing it's best to bind the rope.
You lied.
All I wanted was a proper
dick
down
session.
To be open enough
to receive all of you
—on purpose.
To feel my juices flow down
to the crack of my ass
by way of my inner thigh.
But you lied.
If you had told me you were a dentist
I would have asked you to examine my jaw;
to transform the tip of your dick
into an inspection mirror
and massage my tonsils,
reaching deep down
into the pockets of my esophagus
while vacuuming my saliva
—challenging me to keep it sloppy.
I would have asked you to recline the seat
with my head down and ass waist high
—if you hadn't lied.

June

I felt naked and stripped of my jewels.
Spiraling down the slopes
of disappointment and shame,
my life crumbled like a stale cookie
upon human touch.
A sequence of events
linked by the chain of devastation.
Here I am,
prematurely exposed
to uncontrollable heartache;
vomiting until the end of my days
as an unplanned parent
of someone or something
the doctor says has no chance of survival
—no chance to breathe life
beyond the surface of my womb.
My mind is a maze that a lab rat couldn't complete.
What good is the wealth of knowledge
when it's not applied?
I know what to do and still, I am broken
in a shattered state of mind.
Selling self in high range,
yet consistently devalued,
lied to and/or choosing to believe
what I hear versus what I see.
Warming up my sheets

Pink Gems   *Formidable*

for dreams of family as so it was sold
—wrapped in ribbons of uncertainty.
The cost of discounted pleasure
has been paid for with my dignity.
I ate the hit to my heart
but the wound to my spirit
came with the unbearable blow
from my mother.
From one parent to another,
I could never.

Pink Gems *Eloquent*

Full Grown

I'm not playing hard to get
when I tell you I'm not interested.
I'm grown
and fully capable of expressing
my wants and needs
as well as my dislikes
and the shit I don't need in my life.
I'm not playing games
when I tell you I'm unavailable.
I'm grown
and my time
is strategically accounted for.
So when I check my calendar
and counteroffer with a different time,
respect that I've considered making time
for you at all.
I'm not acting stuck up
when I tell you I don't touch door handles
in the presence of any man I'm with.
Be it my father, uncle, cousin,
brother or friend.
I'm grown
and feminine enough
to allow myself to be covered
by a strong man.
Patient enough

to wait for opportunities
to present themselves
to me.
I'm not being a bitch
when I unsubscribe to your antics.
I'm grown.
MY desires hit different.
I'm talking about
conversations over tea
in the middle of a garden.
Time—
for puzzles and board games
with an audiobook or podcast
sounding in the background
—after enjoying food
from said garden.
Make no mistakes,
I'm grown.

AmeriKKKa's Sweetheart

I am a deliberate nuisance
to the nerves of those
who know better than
to act on their thoughts.
Those who view me
through a tainted lens
in hopes of doing unto me
as their ancestors
have done to mine.
Men who fetishize
the curves on my body,
the dimples on my lower back,
and the warm undertone of my skin.
Women who can't seem to understand
my intelligence—
seeing as though they've had a head start
of about 400 years.
Women who slam doors in my face
and mumble under their breaths
about how I should be
somewhere in servitude.
Men who daydream
about holding my King at gunpoint
as they force him to watch
their Klan folk beat and rape me.
I am a deliberate nuisance

Pink Gems

Spiritual

to the souls of those
who reap the benefits
of oppressors before them.
I speak in the barbaric tongue
and I write as if the ink
comes from the blood of my savior.
I write for the folks before me
who could only accept abuse
as a means for survival.
I write for the souls of our dearly departed
and ask that there be rest
where Zionists have thrived for centuries.
I am a deliberate nuisance
to indoctrinated professionals,
appointed by way of bloodline courtesies.
Folks who wouldn't have degrees
if their names didn't relate
to the names engraved on the buildings.
Folks who prioritize tradition
over peace;
perception over truth;
and arrogance over humility.
I Am a Deliberate Nuisance
to AmeriKKKa.

Heart (Part 2)

Look at me with closed eyes
and see me.
SEE me;
see ME
—See me as vividly
as blind folks see their dreams.
See me like the pattern you can't un-see
once you've discovered it.
Put the 'see me' in semen
and bring forth orgasmic,
authentic love.
Plant your seeds of admiration
into the essence of my beauty
as you see me
Spiritually
Physically
Emotionally
Consistently
Intentionally
Actually
Limitlessly—
See me like high beams
on a country backroad.
—See me with your mind
and unlock the part of me
that can only be seen

Pink Gems   *Queen*

with your third eye.
See me see you see me—
Do you
SEE ME?

Big Guns

I don't feel safe in delicate arms
and sometimes the strong arms
aren't gentle enough to be considered safe.
I need arms that protect in a cuddling state.
Arms with big hands that grip firmly
rather than with uncertainty.
Arms that dissolve all of my insecurities
when wrapped tightly around me.
The kind of arms that bear arms
and are known to not be fucked with.
Arms that beef up and relax slowly
when met by the trace of my fingertips.
Arms that moisten the space
between my legs in the midst
of being embraced.
Arms that penetrate fear
and fuck it to nonexistence.
Arms that break down the barriers
that prevent my femininity
from reaching its peak.
Arms that build fences as opposed
to tearing down walls in our home.
Arms swole enough to lift burdens
and put them in their place.
Arms with knowledge etched into its veins
that are fully capable
of pointing me in the right direction.

These Hands

People would kill to have my hair
as thick as it is
as long as it is
in all of its kinky glory.
Yet, I don't know
what to do with it.
My hands were made for healing
—whatever that means.
From picking up ink pens
and writing letters
that form words of love and pain.
They were made
to craft with paintbrushes
and needles for stitches
and things.
My fingertips are gifts
from the same heaven
that ancestors thrive in
as they watch over me.
These fingertips have brought comfort
to the strongest of men.
They've brought calm
to some of the darkest storms.
Yet, every time
I begin to twist my mane,
my fingers start to cramp.

Pink Gems   *Faithful*

Almost as if they don't belong
between the strands of my tresses.
My fingers have rumbled
with the worst of them
balled up into one mighty fist
after another.
Still, my hair presents a struggle
I've yet to overcome.

High Heels

My toes have a relationship
with the Most High
—separate from the one my spirit has.
On several occasions,
my toes have reached so high
as if reaching for a kiss—
then curled up into itself.
Into me.
Intimacy gravitates to my soul deeply
as your spirit dances with mine.
Only a real gangalae
can lay down the laws in this way.
It takes an unruly lover
to conquer my body
and suspend my legs in the air.
To pry open my lips
and split my walls
upon the veins of your shaft.
You gotta be a bad
mutha-shut-yo-mouth
to silence me
from the burning desire to scream.
My throat wants to holler
for the angels to open up the gates
—my toes are already
halfway there.
Lord...

My Pro-Black is Anti-White

Fuck you thought?
"White" is more than a color.
It's a state of mind.
It symbolizes injustice and inhumanity.
This world is full of crackers.
Saltine crackers.
Graham crackers.
Rice crackers.
The thing that separates us from them
is mentality.
Pink knuckles wrapped around glocks
aimed at unarmed brown backs
nationwide—for sport.
Brown faces in blue uniforms
harassing brown faces on the sidewalks
of inner cities—for brownie points.
Yellow fingertips pointing at brown consumers
and consciously spewing disrespectful
words while demanding a sale.
Ashy knees in blue pants
kneeled into the jugulars of brown necks
with no regard for human life.
Copper bullets slugged
into the chest cavities
of brown men for no real reason.
News coverage—

Pink Gems *Professional*

for everything under the sun
except missing brown women and children.
Stolen organs from brown bodies
sold on the black market
because, white privilege.
Fuck charges.
Time is nigh for retaliation.
Crackers
crumble
under
pressure.

Pink Gems   Assertive

Love's Tongue

When it comes to love languages,
I believe there's more than five.
For instance, SECURITY
is a love language of mine.
Sure TOUCH is my jam;
but if the hands that touch me
are attached to a demon, I want no parts.
If you reach out to hold me with unsteady arms,
don't reach for me at all.
You could reach into your wallet
and buy me gifts all day,
but if you lack ATTENTION TO DETAIL,
you'll miss the mark every time.
QUALITY TIME is deeper
than spending hours at a time
doing nothing together.
We should be making the best
of 30-minute windows.
Tap into your CREATIVITY.
Spoken word sounds good;
but have you ever written a LOVE LETTER
and placed it between the pages
of a book I'm currently reading
or the book we're READING TOGETHER?
I love to hide and seek
handwritten notes on the fridge;

under the pillows;
on the steering wheel;
and amongst c-notes in your wallet.
Love doesn't have to be expensive.
Let me COOK FOR YOU
and you can feed me
in return.
SHOWER ME
with soap in the shower
then fuck me against the tiles
and shower me with affection.
Whisper WORDS OF AFFIRMATION
to me ever so softly,
reminding me every so often
that our love is constant.

Wicked Hour

The part of me that wants to sex you
because sex is just sex
is the same part of me
that's like 'Nah, he don't deserve me.'
But deserving or not,
I still want the D.
So do I move in the spirit of pride
or my vagina's energy?
Cuz she's calling for more
than my fingertips.
She's pleading for more
than silicone dick.
She wants the real thing
and she wants it now.
Rawr
—my pussy is purring
for something real.
Something temporary
and something she can feel.
My pussy is reaching out
on my behalf.
She got me wrestling with wicked thoughts
—arranging meet and greets
to see what's up
—like 'Yeeerrrrrr,
what you up to love?

Pink Gems   Amazing

Are you up for lust?'
She got me out here ready
to spin the block on niggaz
—like 'Hey big head...'

Affirmations for My King

You are exactly the person
the Most High made you to be.
You are strong, beautiful
and more than capable
of protecting and building our nation.
You are not overlooked
or seen as a threat to society.
You are the leader of our tribe.
You are the father of our children.
You are needed.
You are loved.
You are to be served
and cared for hand & foot.
You are my love.
You are my King.
You are sent by my ancestors
to rule alongside me
and carry me to higher heights.
You are love
in its most innocent state
—unashamed,
unafraid.
In this one,
You are life.

The Voice of the Child in Me

The child in me is yearning for my love.
Desperately waiting
for me to shield my own heart
from the naysayers.
I am a Queen.
I am beautiful.
I am more than enough.
I am a bundle of creativity, spice & melanin.
I am fierce.
Passion resides beneath my pores
and glows all over my body.
The child in me screams,
YAAAASSSS Honey!
Show the people who you are.
Tell them what we're all about.
Don't be afraid to open up about our fears.
Be intentional about your presence.
I am the direct ascendant
of trauma and triumph.
I am unconditional love.
I am as priceless as peace
in a chaotic world.
The child in me
will no longer tolerate me
not being myself.
If you don't want me to be who I am,

Pink Gems   *Mentor*

to be the woman the child in me
has empowered me to be,
the child in me wants you to know,
that is too damn bad.

Torn

Skating on the fragile edges
of the ripped sides of this matter,
I have been begging to be heard
but I will not utter a single word
until I am sure of the message I want to convey.
My energy is torn
between the feelings of my heart
and the knowings of my brain
—my spirit has reached the peak of exhaustion.
When will I experience reciprocity?
With that thought
creeps in the notion
of splitting you smooth in half,
but you see,
my anger is precious.
If I give in
to showing you my inner rage,
you will quickly learn that I can cut a tire
down to the rim—
with a butterknife.
You may begin to fear
for what I may do to you
and gather self to do right by me
under false pretense.
And why must we pretend?
You pretend to love me
and I pretend to need you.

God or Nah?

Lord, if I love him religiously,
does that make me a sinner?
If I love him more than I love you,
does that make him my savior?
I love you because you are the creator
of all things. I love him
because he makes me
shake the shake of 1000 earthquakes.
He makes me spill the wetness
of all the oceans combined.
He makes me gasp for air
—even in the rainforest
with more trees than man can count.
He moves mountains of attitude
when I'm stubborn
and want things to go my way.
He makes me call on him
more than I call on you when I pray.
And when I pray,
I always pray that he's coming home to me.
I pray that he's not out there
being a philanthropist
and giving the community
the same loving he gives to me.
I pray that he never finds
a throat deeper than mine.

Pink Gems   *Sacred*

I pray for him more than I pray for me.
Am I broken for loving him more than I love me,
and am I foolish for loving him
more than I love you?

Mic Check

Yes, I'm mature enough
to stand in the same room as you;
to breathe the same air
and be in the same space.
But if you wink at me one more time,
I'm gonna wink back
at the part of you that only has one eye.
And when I do,
I'll need you to be ready.
By that I mean, I want you flaccid
and waiting for me
to give you permission to be aroused.
All growth needs to be because I made it happen.
Are you mature enough to control yourself?
Have you practiced retention long enough
to release only when I say its okay?
I know you thought that you would see me
and remind me of our many mid afternoons
with strung-out hopes
that I would slip you the key to my room.
While I'd love to pretend
to be interested in speaking with you,
I'd rather speak to the mic.

Pink Gems   Unique

Table Top

Don't ask me what I bring to the table
when you invited me
to be your special guest;
and better yet
I have a few questions for you...
What have you prepared for me
to join you at this table?
Is it set for a Queen?
More importantly,
has the table been set
—for me?
When I drink from your glass,
will it be half full
with love, adoration and security?
Or will it be half empty
without a strong foundation to build on?
When I move my hand
to retrieve my salad fork,
wait—is there salad on this table?
Are you intentional
about nourishing my body
and making sure I eat
my share of raw veggies?
Speaking of which,
do you have a garden?
If not, are you prepared to make room

Pink Gems   *Sensitive*

for us to plant,
harvest and feed—together?
As a guest in your world,
what meal have you placed in front of me?
Will I be fulfilled—in all ways—longing for more?
Will I have room for dessert
and energy to run a mile
on nourishment alone?
Will I want to stay?
Cuz see, to have invited me
in the first place
is to KNOW
that I'm prepared to serve;
to nourish;
to uplift;
to relieve;
to assist;
and to BE
the Queen that I have grown to be.
But the question is:
Are you ready for me?

Pink Gems Eclectic

Nah, I'm Good

If being your wife
means placing your needs
next to that of the Most High
and sacrificing damn near all of me for you
—I don't want it.
If it means taking the backseat
to support your ego
while you make deals
and then be expected to go into overdrive
to get us out, if and when the deal backfires
—I don't want it.
If it means always being open to receive you
regardless of any circumstance or feeling
that may arise, I don't want it.
If it means engaging with folks
who do not include or think of me
in the slightest—
if for no other reason than being with you,
I don't want it.
If it means replacing
more of my independent studying
with mindless entertainment
—trading research for hours
in front of the dummy box, I don't want it.
If it means throwing you alley-oops
and also running over to catch and dunk it,

Pink Gems   *Resourceful*

I don't want it.
If it means I'm a bad wife for not praising you
for doing the bare minimum—
and/or something I've asked of you
more than a thousand times,
I DON'T WANT IT.

Brace Thyself

I am standing in the middle of an aisle
at a crowded clothing store,
clutching my pearls and my vagina
because my body remembers
your tender touch
against the backside of my waist.
My body remembers
the firmness of your grip.
My mind replays the sensation.
when my body least expects it;
and at each play,
the sensation grows
stronger than the last one.
My spirit wants me to tell you
that I love you
but my heart has yet to agree.
My cervix is throbbing
for your masculine energy
and while my womb is prepared
to bring seeds to life,
my heart is pleading with my mind
—to wait.
It's not enough
to just appear with warm smiles
and ambitious speeches.
We need more

Pink Gems   *Deep*

than plans sealed with wet kisses.
There's no real future in that.

Pink Gems   Feminine

Short Eyes

Low eyes.
Short eyes.
I'm relearning to trust my intuition;
to not be swayed
by the ink on your skin
tatted by the hands
of an amateur.
The lines aren't as smooth
as your words tend to be.
Supported by the gums
that hold your smile together,
reinforced by the guns in your biceps,
while sending signals to my finger.
Practically begging me to pull the trigger,
aiming between your eyes
and searching your soul
for any sign of passion...
but all I see
is the emptiness I felt
in your space.
Low eyes.
Short eyes.
I'm choosing not to ignore my intuition;
to acknowledge and release my triggers,
giving them voice to breathe life
into my heart's story

Pink Gems   *Productive*

shared by the narrative of my womb
and my soul's recital.
My words seen as glass
from the perspective of your eyes.
You don't hear and you can only see
the mold that you've been sculpting
for someone whom you believe is like me.
Younger in age and mature enough
to be curious about the world as you see it.
Sexy, feminine and feisty enough
to quench your thirst for the chase
—like a fox being cornered by a wolf.
I can see it in your eyes.
Low eyes.
Short eyes.
I'm trusting my intuition.

Pink Gems   *Compassionate*

Necessary Roughness

Push my leg up on the counter
in front of the mirror
—watch the expressions
on my face as you slowly slide in.
Place your strong hand
around my neck,
nibble on my earlobe
and give it to me hard.
Increase your speed
then pull out.
Sit my ass on the counter.
Drop down and put your tongue
where it belongs.
One lick
two licks.
Pick me up
to straddle that big ol' dick.
My titties will bounce
and I can touch the ceiling.
Pull out.
Hug me and breathe.
Fuck me
between my thighs.
Carry me to the couch
and toss me on my side.
Thrust me from here

Pink Gems   *Witty*

while kissing my lips
and tugging at my nipples.
Twist them counter-clockwise
with both hands;
rotating my nipples and lips
onto yours.
Pull out.
Swing your nut sack
over my nose
and enter
your second favorite hole.
Gag me with the sweet taste
of myself all over you.

Love Rising

I've been waiting all night
to say good morning to you
and what a grand rising
it shall be.
I've been thinking about you
in my dreams.
Feening to glide my warm tongue
all over your chest.
Exploring skin cells
that haven't met me yet.
Kissing the parts
you often hide from the world.
Tracing my fingers
along the trail of my wetness,
I take you whole
into my cheeks.
Breakfast is served
and you're awake
from your sleep.
I feel your hand
massaging the top of my head
and I slowly pull up
to meet your eyes and wink.
I love it when you stare at me,
balls deep into my chin.
You always taste so good to me.

Pink Gems   *Exceptional*

Tourmaline

I have traveled to many places
since I was found
lingering on the shores
of a Kenyan lake.
Now, here I am
on the ledge of someone's balcony
drowning in fresh rain water.
The best part about being here
is the light that comes to shine on me
every so often.
Something about being under the full moon
leaves me shiny and recharged.
It's the feeling of counting stars
with one's true love.
Of all the many places I've been,
the ledge is my favorite.
Fully immersed
into the truest form of nature,
I am blessed
to finally have caring hands.
I thought so many years ago
that I would only be picked up
and thrown away—yet, here I am
on this ledge bathing
under my second full moon this year.

Pink Gems · Supportive

Deeper

I don't want you to lust for me.
I want you to develop love for me
and love me thoroughly
from the spirit of your soul.
Love me uncovered
and unashamed.
I've unpacked my bags,
worked through my shit
and discarded things
that no longer served me
—all before you got here.
The things I still have
are too heavy for me to carry alone;
too heavy for me to move on my own.
—Light work for the man who loves me.
Strong enough to take my bag
and move it to the curb
the night before trash day.
Wise enough to show me
that letting go requires
the mighty hands of the man
my ancestors
and The Most High;
sent to lay on me.
Love me in action
and with great intention

Pink Gems   *Brooklynite*

while serving as the head
to my body.
Lead me
so that I can keep you
uplifted
respected
admired
and loved in return
—naked.
All lust aside.

Pink Gems   *Provocative*

Shadow Work

When you turn to the streets
because it feels better
to be dissed by strangers
than flesh and blood,
Sis, I see you.
Walking through alleys
with the shadows of pimps
lurking closely behind,
I see the different types of pain
in your tears that damn near burns
through your cheeks and quickly dries
in the air of this cold world.
I see you holding onto pain
and discounting your worth.
I see you reluctant to accept help
from smiling strangers
because changes have never truly
been in your favor.
I see the cops with their dicks out
and other public servants
with phony handouts as they sign
their names into your dismay.
I see you when you feel unloved
in rooms filled with people
who love you.
It's the same feeling you get

Pink Gems   *Focused*

when you realize that the one
you love most may as well be
as far from you as the moon.
I see you.
Take the time you need
to think the thoughts
that enter your mind.
Process them with care
and allow yourself to live in the moment.
Be in the space of looking into yourself
as you remember the folks
who had you fucked up.
Feel the emotions
you experienced and then imagine
a different outcome for yourself.
One that you will be proud of—or not.
An outcome that makes you
feel better today than you did that day.
Replay the script in your mind
or recite it aloud in private.
The narrative is yours
to alter however you see fit.
Move on, knowing
that what you've been through
shields you from the bullshit to come.

Show and Prove

For me to be soft,
I need to relax.
For me to relax,
I need to be able to trust you.
For me to trust you,
I need to know you got it.
For me to know you got it,
I need to see proof.
For me to see proof,
I need you to show results.
For you to show results,
you need to execute
your verbal commitments.
Do what the fuck you say
you're gonna do.
Exceed my expectations.
It is not too much
to want to be prepared for
with the same level of energy
that I give off to nurture.
It is not too high
of an expectation to be respected,
valued and genuinely looked after.
It is not unreasonable
to want the support of someone
that I can bet on as sure

Pink Gems *Whole*

as I can bet on myself.
It is absolutely absurd
for you to think you should
have access to my time
my body
my heart
my mind
my inner being
my womb
and my future
—while only offering the bare minimum
to foot the bill of effort.

Eye Opener

Pull ya back ya hood so I can look at you.
Place my nipples between
your fingers and twist.
I see, I see...Mmm
I see you filling out nicely into yourself.
Got me looking at un-snipped flesh
in a whole new light.
I see you see me
with that one eye open.
I see the beginning of a perfect greeting
between tongue and glans.

User Error

It was a mistake,
but I have to thank you
for some of the best head
I've ever received.
I mean, your tongue moved
about like a jump drive
injected into my brain's hard drive.
It was like you downloaded every thought
I ever had about anything
pertaining to ultimate pleasure.
And who am I to be surprised?
I should've known
that from the moment you winked at me
with that lustful sparkle
in your eye, that I would
soon be bent over with a demon
between my thighs.
Your tongue thrusted into me
and searched my walls for hidden data.
That long thang
penetrated me like a virus
and took over all my shit.
Like I couldn't feel my toes
but in the back of my mind,
I knew they had curled a few times over.
My body twisted

Pink Gems   *Outspoken*

to the rhythm of your strokes.
I tried to scream and call out
to let you know what you already knew
but my voice box was missing.
Like a stolen possession.
Yes, it was a mistake
—just like the other 12 times,
but I won't make it again.
This lustful cycle of ours
is costing me my soul.
I've got to shut it down.

Breathing Room

When I tell you I need space,
it doesn't mean I don't want you to be near.
I don't want you to pack up your dick and leave.
See, what I really mean is
I need space to exist
without your voice in my ears
asking questions to spark unnecessary conversations.
I need enough space to pass gas
without having to excuse myself,
cuz you're so close you might smell it.
My need for space
doesn't mean we can't be in the same room.
It just means that you should be
doing what you do while I'm focused
on the things that interest me.
Two people occupying the same space
yet in their own worlds.
Close enough for footsies
but with enough breathing room
to not feel smothered.
My love, trust me when I say,
I don't want you to pack up your dick and leave.
I just need a little bit more space
so I can breathe.

Commencement

The time has come
for me to be responsible
with my blessings,
my gifts, my talents
and my choices.
I owe it to myself
to prove to myself
I've learned the lessons
that I've been too hardheaded
and stiff-necked to have learned
the first time around.
Too big-hearted to not adhere
to the advice of the folks who tried
to talk me out of my own self-destruction.
The same folks who tried to convince me
that love is a fairytale I made up in my head.
It is merely a campaign
for my heart's desires to prevail
against the logic in my brain.
My heart has won this race
time and time again, but now
the time has come for change.
I owe it to myself to lead
with the thoughts of a woman with degrees.
An associates in Not This Time, Playa;
a bachelor's in Get Your Life;

Pink Gems *Sassy*

a master's in I Said What I Said
and a phd in Committed to Peace.
I've unpacked my trauma
and now I'm not living
with the shit I've carried for years.
It's a newfound freedom.
I've gotten to know myself for myself.
I accept myself as myself
and I fuck with me, heavy.
I've always known
that I was the shit but now,
I'm not trauma-bonding with myself.
I'm loving on me
from a space of peace.
I've forgiven myself and others
for trespassing against my spirit.
I'm reminded by folks who love me
that I don't have to be everything
in order to be in the presence of being.
Being in the now.
Being as I am.
Being.
Breathing.
Seeing.
Living.

Haiku Series

Pink Gems   Phenomenal

Dead Weight

Your assertive hands
caressing my waist, feels like
love—before the pain.

Thin Line

Your tongue down my throat
indicates that we are close
—even as strangers.

Conception

Pulsating pussy.
Cum in to know me, and then
claim your legacy.

Round Up

In order for me
to reach peaks higher than high,
you need eight—at least.

Pink Gems   Articulate

Precision

Lick me from the front.
Penetrate me from the back.
Finish me with love.

Sign Language

Nipples through my shirt,
speaking louder than my voice.
Holla if you heard!

Candy Man

Pre-cum bubblegum,
I'm finna blow you tonight
and pop it one time.

Glisten

My coochie is bare
—as hairless as a baldie.
Come spit shine her up.

Envy

Part your lips and place
them on mine. Make the left lip
jealous of the right.

Speak It

Consent is a must.
Speak up and say what you want.
Make it crystal clear.

Intention

Lusty energy
creates the false narrative
of genuine care.

Blemished Rose

My scars are roadmaps
to the trauma I've endured.
Still, I am worthy.

Uninhibited

I'll fuck if I want
and if so, I'll let you know.
No pressure needed.

Alpha Moves

Keep what you're about
to do to your fuckin self.
Do it first, then share.

Prelude

Kissing warms my heart.
It's like sex before the sex.
Don't stop kissing me.

Towel Down

All red lights are not
created equally. This
one's meant to be ran.

First & Foremost

Tell me what to do,
if you can. What happens next
will tell you what's true.

Take Ownership

My pussy's ready
for you to engrave your name
all up and through her.

On My Way

Caressing myself,
wishing it was you instead.
I'll be cumming soon.

Peace Out

If you fold under
pressure, you are not the one.
Respectfully, Me.

Pink Gems *Empress*

Joint Effort

Strong leadership will grant submission from me. But not dictatorship.

Layers

Getting dicked-down with consent to be choked out is a form of self-care.

Thank You

You stimulate my mind in ways that inspire me to be better.

Thank you for traveling this journey with me!
I hope that you use my lessons as a guide to learn more about yourself.

Reflect on where you've been
and channel that into who you are now.

Release what needs to go.

TAKE UP SPACE.

Whenever you find yourself
tripping over the bar you've set for self,
raise it.

Love Always,

Dominique D. Glisson
ButtaFlyy ~ Kahawia

More from the Author

Pink Canvas

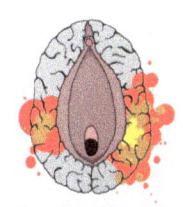

Dominique D. Glisson

Pink Canvas

A collection of poems written for any woman seeking love through her reproductive organs. Pink Canvas vividly captures the thoughts of a woman battling with vaginal power, seduction, lust, love, abstinence and self-worth.

Pink Lotus

A collection of poems written for the healing process of any woman who has her vagina in her heart's position. Developed from Pink Canvas, Pink Lotus continues the journey toward vaginal power, seduction and self-worth.

Pink Lotus

Dominique D. Glisson

I Got Time Today!

The must-have journal for writers of color who are struggling to get over a case of Writer's Block. It includes more than 50 prompts, created to provoke thought and inspire your creative juices to overflow.

K & K Podcast: Real Talk w/ Kiva & Kahawia

Two ladies having real discussions about life, womanhood and love through literature. We read to understand. We speak to empower. We are Kiva and Kahawia.

AfroSoFly.com

Patreon.com/AfroSoFly

IG: _afrosofly

IG: kahawia__

Kahawia.com

www.ingramcontent.com/pod-product-compliance
Lightning Source LLC
Chambersburg PA
CBHW061731070526
44583CB00024B/3093